Understanding Large Language Models: A Guide to

Transformer Architectures and NLP Applications

Contents

Part 1: Introduction

Welcome to the wondrous world of language! This part of the book sets the stage for our exploration of Large Language Models (LLMs) and the transformative power they hold.

Chapter 1: The Power of Language: A Dive into Natural Language Processing (NLP)

Language is the cornerstone of human communication. It allows us to share ideas, express emotions, and build connections. But for computers, deciphering the complexities of human language has long been a challenge. This is where Natural Language Processing (NLP) steps in.

- **1.1 The Rise of NLP and its Applications:**

  Imagine a world where computers can understand and respond to our natural language. NLP is making this dream a reality. We'll delve into the exciting rise of NLP and explore its vast applications. From chatbots that answer your questions to machine translation that breaks down language barriers, NLP is revolutionizing the way we interact with technology.

- **1.2 Challenges of Natural Language Processing:**

  However, NLP isn't all sunshine and rainbows. Language is messy, ambiguous, and constantly evolving. We'll explore the inherent challenges of NLP, such as understanding sarcasm, deciphering slang, and dealing with the ever-

growing vocabulary humans use.

Chapter 2: Unveiling Large Language Models (LLMs)

Now, let's introduce the game-changers: Large Language Models (LLMs). These are powerful AI models trained on massive amounts of text data. Think books, articles, code, and even the vast information highway of the internet!

- **2.1 What are LLMs and How Do They Work?:** This chapter will unveil the inner workings of LLMs. We'll break down their core concepts and see how they learn from mountains of text data. You'll discover how LLMs can generate human-quality text, translate languages, and answer your questions in an informative way.

- **2.2 The Impact of LLMs on Various Industries:** Get ready to be amazed! LLMs are having a profound impact on various industries. We'll explore how they are transforming fields like customer service, content creation, and even scientific research. Imagine a world where AI can write compelling marketing copy, summarize complex research papers, or even create engaging stories – that's the power of LLMs!

- **2.3 Limitations and Ethical Considerations of LLMs:** As with any powerful technology, there are limitations and ethical considerations to address. We'll discuss the potential biases that LLMs might inherit from the data they're trained on. We'll also explore issues like transparency and accountability in the development and use of LLMs.

By understanding these limitations and fostering responsible development, we can ensure that LLMs become a force for good in the world.

This opening section provides a foundation for understanding LLMs and their place within the NLP landscape. The following chapters will delve deeper into the technical aspects of transformers, the key architecture powering LLMs, and their far-reaching applications.

Part 2: Foundations for Understanding LLMs

Before we dive into the revolutionary world of

transformer architectures, let's build a solid

foundation. This part equips you with the key

concepts that pave the way for understanding Large

Language Models (LLMs).

Chapter 3: Deep Learning Essentials for NLP

Imagine the human brain, a complex network of

neurons that allows us to learn and process

information. Deep learning takes inspiration from this biological marvel.

- **3.1 Introduction to Neural Networks for Language Processing:** In this chapter, we'll explore how deep learning neural networks are used for NLP tasks. We'll break down the basic structure of these networks and see how they learn from data to perform tasks like text classification or sentiment analysis.

- **3.2 Understanding Recurrent Neural Networks (RNNs):** One prominent type of neural network for NLP is the Recurrent Neural Network (RNN). RNNs are particularly adept at handling sequential data, like sentences or paragraphs.

We'll delve into how RNNs process information one step at a time, allowing them to capture the context within language.

- **3.3 Limitations of RNNs and the Need for New Architectures:** While RNNs were a breakthrough, they have limitations. Processing long sequences can be challenging for them. This chapter will explore these limitations and introduce the need for a new architecture – the transformer – that will become the game-changer for LLMs.

Chapter 4: Breaking Down the Hype: Traditional NLP Techniques

Before transformers came along, NLP relied on some powerful traditional techniques. Understanding these techniques provides valuable context for the advancements transformers bring.

- **4.1 Word Embeddings and Capturing Meaning in Language:** Words are the building blocks of language, but computers don't understand them inherently. Word embeddings come to the rescue! We'll explore how these techniques represent words numerically, capturing the relationships between words and their meaning within a larger context.

- **4.2 Language Modeling: Understanding Sequential Text Data:** Language modeling is a fundamental concept in NLP. It involves predicting the next word in a sequence, allowing us to understand the statistical relationships between words. This chapter delves into different language modeling techniques and how they help computers grasp the flow and structure of language.

- **4.3 Sequence-to-Sequence Learning for Tasks like Machine Translation:** Imagine translating a sentence from one language to another. Sequence-to-sequence learning models tackle this challenge. We'll explore how these models process an input sequence (e.g., a sentence in English) and generate a corresponding output sequence (e.g., the translated sentence in Spanish).

By understanding these traditional NLP techniques, you'll gain a deeper appreciation for the innovations that transformer architectures bring to the table. The next part will unveil the secrets behind transformers

and how they revolutionized the world of LLMs.

Part 3: The Transformer Revolution

Brace yourself for a paradigm shift! This part introduces transformers, the revolutionary architecture that underpins Large Language Models (LLMs). Get ready to understand how transformers have transformed the way computers process and generate human language.

Chapter 5: Unveiling the Transformer Architecture: A Paradigm Shift

Before transformers, NLP relied on techniques like RNNs. While powerful, they had limitations. Enter the transformer – a new architecture that broke the mold.

- **5.1 Core Principles of the Transformer Model:** This chapter dives into the core principles of transformers. We'll explore how they differ from RNNs and introduce the concept of self-attention, a game-changing mechanism that allows transformers to understand long-range relationships within text.

- **5.2 Encoder-Decoder Structure: Decoding Language Step-by-Step:** Transformers, like some traditional NLP techniques, follow an encoder-decoder structure. We'll break down how the encoder processes the input text, capturing its meaning, and how the decoder uses this information to generate the output, like translating a sentence or writing a creative text format.

- **5.3 The Power of Attention: Understanding Relationships in Text:** Attention is the secret sauce of transformers! This chapter delves into the concept of attention and how it allows the model to focus on specific parts of the input text that are relevant to the current task. Imagine reading a sentence and paying close attention to the key words to understand its meaning – that's what attention does in transformers!

- **5.4 Benefits of Transformers: Speed, Accuracy, and Long-Range Dependencies:** Transformers offer several advantages over traditional NLP techniques. We'll explore how their parallel processing capabilities make them faster, how their attention mechanism improves accuracy, and how they can capture long-range dependencies in language, leading to a more nuanced understanding of text.

Chapter 6: Exploring Variations of the Transformer Architecture

The transformer architecture is like a powerful engine, and just like car engines have different models, transformers have variations too!

- **6.1 Understanding Different Transformer Variants (e.g., BERT, GPT):** This chapter introduces you to some of the most popular transformer variants, like BERT and GPT. We'll explore how these variants are built upon the core transformer architecture but are fine-tuned for specific NLP tasks. For instance, BERT excels at understanding complex queries, while GPT is a whiz at generating creative text formats.

- **6.2 How Transformer Variants are Tailored for Specific NLP Tasks:** We'll delve into how the strengths of different transformer variants are leveraged for various tasks. Imagine using a specialized tool for each job – that's the idea behind having transformer variants tailored to specific NLP applications.

By understanding the transformer architecture and its variations, you'll gain a deeper appreciation for the advancements in NLP and how LLMs are pushing the boundaries of what computers can do with language. The next part will bridge the gap between theory and practice, exploring how LLMs are trained and the vast applications they hold.

The Transformer Architecture: Beyond Attention Mechanisms

The Transformer architecture, first introduced in the 2017 paper *Attention is All You Need* by Vaswani et al., has fundamentally reshaped the landscape of Natural

Language Processing (NLP). At its core, the Transformer is based on self-attention mechanisms, which allow a model to attend to all positions in an input sequence simultaneously, rather than sequentially processing tokens as done in Recurrent Neural Networks (RNNs) or Long Short-Term Memory (LSTM) networks. This parallelism allows for more efficient training, as computations can be performed simultaneously across the sequence.

The architecture consists of an encoder-decoder structure, both of which rely heavily on multi-head self-attention mechanisms. These attention layers allow the model to compute relationships between tokens, capturing both short-range and long-range dependencies. Multi-head attention extends this by using several attention heads to learn multiple relationships at different levels of abstraction, which enhances the model's ability to capture nuanced meanings in text.

While the original Transformer introduced the self-attention mechanism, its true power has been realized through adaptations and modifications. For instance, BERT and GPT, two of the most popular models built on Transformer principles, have different takes on architecture. BERT (Bidirectional Encoder Representations from Transformers) leverages only the encoder for masked language modeling, making it more adept at tasks requiring context understanding like question answering and classification. In contrast, GPT (Generative Pretrained Transformer) relies on a decoder-based structure, excelling in text generation and completion tasks.

While these models have become foundational in NLP, there are several challenges that remain. One major issue is the computational cost. The quadratic complexity of attention mechanisms with respect to sequence length makes scaling Transformer models to very long sequences computationally expensive. Researchers have proposed solutions such as sparse attention (Reformer) and memory-augmented attention (Linformer), which aim to reduce this complexity without compromising the model's ability to learn long-range dependencies.

Another challenge is the issue of model explainability. Transformers, by design, lack the inherent structure that RNNs provide, which makes understanding how they make decisions more difficult. This black-box nature has led to growing concerns, particularly in high-stakes applications like healthcare or law, where model decisions need to be transparent and interpretable.

Despite these challenges, Transformer architectures are continuously evolving, with innovations in efficiency and scalability, including more sophisticated methods of parameter sharing, architectural modifications for better handling of longer sequences, and methods to improve the model's ability to reason about complex, structured information.

Scaling Transformers: Innovations and Challenges in Large-Scale Models

The success of large Transformer models such as GPT-3, with its 175 billion parameters, has prompted researchers to explore the limits of scaling. Scaling models has been shown to result in improved performance, especially when tackling complex tasks or operating in a zero-shot or few-shot learning context. Larger models often outperform smaller ones on standard NLP benchmarks, demonstrating an increasing ability to generalize across tasks.

However, scaling up Transformer models is not without its challenges. The most significant hurdle is computational cost. Training large models requires enormous amounts of data and computational power, typically across hundreds or thousands of GPUs or TPUs. This has led to the centralization of large-scale model development in a few well-funded institutions, which raises concerns about the accessibility of these models for researchers with fewer resources.

To mitigate these issues, several techniques have been developed to make training large models more efficient. Mixed-precision training, for example, allows models to use less memory and process more data by using lower-precision data types, such as FP16 instead of FP32. Gradient checkpointing is another technique that reduces memory usage during training by saving intermediate states only at certain intervals, thus reducing the overall memory footprint. These optimizations, along with efficient distributed training frameworks, have made it possible to train extremely large models across multiple devices.

In addition to hardware optimizations, architectural innovations have played a critical role in scaling Transformer models. For example, models like T5 and DeBERTa introduce modifications to the original Transformer architecture to increase efficiency and improve performance. DeBERTa, for instance, introduces disentangled attention mechanisms that enable the model to better capture fine-grained relationships between tokens, leading to improvements in tasks like sentence pair classification and natural language inference.

Another key aspect of scaling is the increase in the amount of data used for pre-training. Models like GPT-3 have been trained on hundreds of billions of tokens, allowing them to learn general representations of language that can be fine-tuned for specific tasks. The use of massive datasets, however, raises ethical concerns. Training models on vast amounts of publicly available text data can inadvertently reinforce societal biases or learn harmful stereotypes, making it crucial to address bias during pre-training and fine-tuning processes.

While scaling has resulted in remarkable advancements, there is a growing recognition that model size is not the only determinant of performance. Innovations in data efficiency, better utilization of pre-trained models, and the development of more specialized models are beginning to show that scaling may need to be complemented with more intelligent approaches to model training and optimization.

Efficient Transformers: Handling Long-Range Dependencies

One of the key innovations in Transformers was their ability to capture long-range dependencies in text. However, the quadratic complexity of self-attention, where each token must attend to every other token, creates significant challenges when dealing with very long sequences. As a result, researchers have worked on numerous methods to improve Transformer efficiency in processing long-range dependencies.

Reformer, introduced by Nikita Kitaev et al., is one of the most notable models in this area. It reduces the quadratic complexity of the original Transformer by using locality-sensitive hashing (LSH) to identify similar tokens within a sequence, thus reducing the number of attention calculations required. By grouping tokens that are highly similar and only computing attention between them, Reformer can handle longer sequences more efficiently without compromising the quality of the learned representations.

Another approach to improving Transformer efficiency is the use of sparse attention mechanisms. Models like the Longformer utilize a sliding window attention mechanism, where each token only attends to its local context, significantly reducing the computational burden. By also incorporating global attention for a subset of tokens, such as those representing special tokens like [CLS] in BERT or [SEP] in T5, Longformer can strike a balance between local and global context, enabling it to scale to longer sequences while maintaining a reasonable computational cost.

The Linformer, another efficient variant, approximates the full attention mechanism by reducing the number of attention heads. It relies on low-rank matrix approximations to reduce the complexity of the attention matrix. This allows Linformer to process long sequences more efficiently while still capturing the essential relationships between tokens in the sequence.

These efficient Transformer variants, though successful in reducing computational cost, come with trade-offs. Some, like Reformer, may sacrifice the model's ability to capture very fine-grained relationships in sequences, while others, like Longformer, must strike a balance between long-range and short-range dependencies. Despite these trade-offs, the development of efficient Transformers is an active area of research, as the demand for handling longer documents or continuous text in real-time applications grows.

Advanced Fine-Tuning and Transfer Learning in LLMs

Fine-tuning pre-trained large language models (LLMs) on task-specific data is an essential part of making these models applicable to real-world problems. While pre-training enables LLMs to acquire a broad understanding of language, fine-tuning allows these models to specialize in specific tasks, such as text classification, question answering, or even code generation.

One of the breakthroughs in LLM fine-tuning is the ability to adapt models like GPT and BERT to a wide variety of tasks with minimal task-specific training data. This ability is made possible by transfer learning, where a model that has been pre-trained on a massive corpus is adapted to a new task by continuing its training on smaller, task-specific datasets. Fine-tuning a model like BERT can often lead to significant improvements in performance with relatively little data, making LLMs highly efficient for applications in domains with limited labeled datasets.

However, fine-tuning LLMs comes with challenges, particularly when dealing with domain-specific applications. For instance, models pre-trained on general-purpose corpora may struggle to understand domain-specific jargon or contextual nuances found in specialized fields like law or medicine. To address this, domain-adaptive fine-tuning techniques have been developed, where LLMs are fine-tuned on data from specific domains before they are further tuned for a particular task. This helps the model learn both domain-specific vocabulary and task-specific patterns.

Furthermore, the process of fine-tuning can be computationally expensive, particularly for large models. Recent work has focused on techniques to reduce the computational cost of fine-tuning while maintaining high performance. Few-shot and zero-shot learning, popularized by GPT-3, allow models to generalize to tasks without needing explicit fine-tuning on those tasks. By leveraging few-shot or zero-shot learning, models can perform well on a variety of tasks by conditioning on a small number of task-specific examples or instructions provided in the input.

Another important avenue of research is the exploration of transfer learning in multi-task settings. Multi-task learning, where a model is trained on several tasks simultaneously, can help improve the generalization ability of the model and enable it to learn shared representations that benefit all tasks. Recent advancements in multi-task learning frameworks have made it possible to train LLMs on a combination of supervised and unsupervised tasks, improving their ability to handle diverse linguistic phenomena and complex applications.

Ethical Considerations in Large Language Models

As large-scale models like GPT-3 continue to push the boundaries of what is possible in NLP, ethical concerns around their development and deployment have become increasingly prominent. One of the most pressing issues is the potential for bias in LLMs. These models are often trained on vast corpora of text scraped from the internet, which inevitably includes biased, offensive, or discriminatory content. Without careful filtering, these biases can be learned by the model and perpetuated in its outputs.

Researchers have made significant strides in developing methods to mitigate bias in LLMs. One approach is to curate training data more carefully, ensuring that it is diverse, representative, and free from harmful stereotypes. Another approach is to fine-tune models using de-biasing techniques, such as adversarial training, where the model is penalized for generating biased outputs. Other methods, like prompt engineering, allow users to guide models towards more ethical responses by adjusting the way queries are phrased.

Transparency and accountability are other key ethical considerations in LLM development. Given the complexity and opacity of these models, it is often difficult for users to understand how a particular output was generated or to trace the decision-making process behind a model's predictions. Researchers have called for increased transparency in model development, including the release of training data, model architecture details, and performance evaluations. There is also growing interest in the development of tools that can explain the reasoning behind model decisions, making LLMs more interpretable and trustworthy for high-stakes applications.

Moreover, concerns about misinformation and the misuse of LLMs for malicious purposes, such as generating deepfakes or automating disinformation campaigns, have raised alarms. Researchers and policymakers alike are exploring ways to address these risks, including the development of safeguards, content moderation systems, and ethical guidelines for the deployment of generative models.

As the use of LLMs continues to grow, it is crucial that ethical considerations are integrated into every stage of model development and deployment. From addressing bias to ensuring transparency and mitigating misuse, it is imperative that the AI community works together to ensure these powerful tools are used responsibly.

Scaling Transformers for Multimodal Learning

Multimodal learning has emerged as one of the most exciting frontiers in deep learning, especially with the rise of multimodal transformers that can process not only text but also images, video, and even audio. The fusion of multiple data types opens up new possibilities for applications ranging from autonomous driving to enhanced content creation. The idea of combining different modalities into a unified model stems from the understanding that real-world data is often multimodal in nature, where information in one modality (e.g., images) can complement and enrich the understanding of another (e.g., text).

Transformers, with their self-attention mechanism, have proven to be highly effective in capturing relationships across modalities. Models like Vision Transformer (ViT) and CLIP (Contrastive Language-Image Pretraining) represent the state-of-the-art in visual and textual fusion. CLIP, for example, learns to map both images and text into a shared embedding space, making it possible to retrieve images based on textual queries or generate descriptive text from images.

The most powerful multimodal models, such as GPT-4 and DALL·E, further expand this capability by enabling the generation of both text and images from a single input. These models use a combination of a Transformer backbone for text generation and specialized layers for processing and generating visual content. The process typically involves mapping both image pixels and text tokens to a shared latent space where cross-modal attention mechanisms allow for joint reasoning between modalities.

However, multimodal learning is not without its challenges. The key hurdle in multimodal transformers is aligning information from different modalities. Text and images, for example, are represented very differently in their raw formats, with text being sequential and discrete, while images are continuous and often contain highly structured spatial information. Handling this disparity requires sophisticated architectural modifications, such as the use of vision transformers for processing image data and specialized fusion layers that combine information from both domains.

Another challenge is computational efficiency. Multimodal models tend to have significantly larger parameter counts compared to unimodal models due to the need to handle multiple data types simultaneously. Efficient model training techniques, like transfer learning from pretrained unimodal models, can help alleviate the computational burden, but it still remains a key area of research. Methods like cross-attention or early fusion strategies, where modality-specific features are merged at various points in the network, are explored to streamline the training process.

In the future, multimodal transformers hold great promise for applications such as enhanced virtual assistants, automated video generation, and even more interactive and responsive AI systems capable of interpreting complex, multimodal inputs. The fusion of multiple modalities is expected to enable richer understanding and creativity in AI, paving the way for more human-like AI systems.

Advanced Fine-Tuning Strategies for Specialized Tasks

Fine-tuning pre-trained large language models (LLMs) is an essential part of customizing these models for specific tasks and domains. The effectiveness of fine-tuning depends not only on the architecture but also on how the pre-trained model is adapted to a new task or domain. This process can be optimized in several ways to improve task-specific performance while minimizing the need for extensive computational resources.

Traditional fine-tuning involves updating all the parameters of a pre-trained model on a smaller, task-specific dataset. This approach works well when the dataset is large and contains domain-relevant data. However, fine-tuning large models, particularly those with billions of parameters, is computationally expensive and requires access to powerful hardware. As a result, several more efficient fine-tuning strategies have been developed to address these challenges.

One of the most popular strategies is **adapter tuning**, where small modules, or "adapters," are inserted between the layers of the pre-trained model. These adapters are fine-tuned on the task-specific data, allowing the core of the pre-trained model to remain unchanged. This method drastically reduces the number of parameters that need to be updated, making it more efficient while still allowing for task specialization. For instance, adapters can be trained on domain-specific corpora, enabling the model to learn nuanced representations without having to retrain the entire network.

Another fine-tuning strategy is **prompt-based learning**, which leverages the power of pre-trained models without requiring full fine-tuning. In this approach, the model is provided with specially crafted prompts that guide it to perform specific tasks. This technique takes advantage of the fact that many large models, like GPT-3, already have a strong ability to generalize and can perform many tasks with minimal task-specific training. With well-designed prompts, models can be conditioned to produce the desired output, even with little or no retraining.

In some scenarios, **few-shot learning** has become a practical approach for adapting large models to specialized tasks. Few-shot learning leverages a small number of labeled examples to adapt a model quickly to a new task. In contrast to traditional supervised learning, where a large amount of labeled data is required, few-shot learning is particularly useful in domains with limited data availability, such as medical or legal applications. Few-shot learning often works in conjunction with prompt-based learning, where a few example tasks are included within the input to guide the model's output.

Moreover, **knowledge distillation** is another advanced fine-tuning technique used to compress large models into smaller, more efficient ones without sacrificing much performance. Knowledge distillation works by training a smaller student model to mimic the behavior of a larger teacher model, which allows the student to achieve similar performance while having fewer parameters.

Finally, **domain-specific fine-tuning** techniques have been developed to address specific nuances in different industries. For example, fine-tuning a language model on legal or medical data requires ensuring the model understands the unique jargon, abbreviations, and complex relationships inherent in these fields. Specialized tokenizers, domain-specific pre-training, and custom loss functions can be employed to help the model better adapt to domain-specific challenges.

Transformers in Cross-Lingual Understanding and Multilingual Models

The advent of large-scale pre-trained language models has significantly impacted the field of cross-lingual understanding, enabling models to perform well across multiple languages with minimal task-specific data. These multilingual and cross-lingual models, which include mBERT (Multilingual BERT) and XLM-R (Cross-lingual RoBERTa), are capable of understanding and generating text in multiple languages without needing to be retrained for each language.

One of the key innovations in this area is the ability of these models to learn shared representations that can be leveraged across languages. This is particularly important for tasks like translation, question answering, and text classification, where training data may be scarce for some languages but abundant for others. Cross-lingual models address this issue by allowing knowledge learned from high-resource languages (such as English) to be transferred to low-resource languages (such as Swahili or Tagalog).

While multilingual models have shown impressive performance, there are significant challenges in this area. The main challenge is the **language imbalance problem**, where some languages have much more training data than others. For instance, English has vast corpora available for training, whereas languages like Yoruba or Xhosa have significantly less data available. To mitigate this, techniques like **data augmentation** are used to synthetically expand the training data for low-resource languages. These techniques include back-translation, where sentences are translated into another language and then back into the original language, creating additional training examples.

Another important challenge is the **language interference problem**, where a multilingual model may confuse words or concepts from one language with those from another, leading to performance degradation. For example, a model trained on both French and English may struggle with homophones or similar words that exist in both languages but have different meanings. This issue is often addressed by using techniques like **language identification** at the input level to ensure that the model correctly understands which language it is processing and adjusts its parameters accordingly.

In addition to multilingual models, **zero-shot translation** has become an area of focus. Zero-shot models, such as mBART and MASS, allow for translation between languages without any direct parallel training data. Instead, these models leverage a shared multilingual representation learned during pre-training and apply this knowledge to translate between languages that were not part of the training corpus.

Despite their successes, multilingual models are still an area of active research, particularly in the domain of low-resource languages. The goal is to improve performance for languages with limited data while reducing the computational cost of maintaining and training separate models for each language.

Transformer Architectures for Code Generation and Program Synthesis

In recent years, Transformer models have been successfully applied to the domain of code generation and program synthesis, areas where understanding logic, syntax, and semantics is crucial. Code generation involves the automatic creation of code snippets or entire programs based on high-level descriptions or specific inputs, while program synthesis involves generating programs that meet particular specifications or requirements.

Models like OpenAI's Codex (the model behind GitHub Copilot) have demonstrated the ability to generate high-quality code in multiple programming languages, including Python, JavaScript, and C++. These models are typically trained on vast codebases from open-source repositories, where they learn to generate syntactically correct and semantically meaningful code based on user input.

The success of code generation using Transformers can be attributed to their ability to model the sequential nature of programming languages, capturing both syntax and semantics. By using a pre-trained language model that has been fine-tuned on code, these models can perform tasks such as autocompletion, bug detection, refactoring, and even translating code from one programming language to another.

In addition to code generation, Transformers have shown promise in **program synthesis** tasks, where the goal is to generate a program from a formal specification. For example, models like GPT-3 and T5 have been used to generate code based on natural language descriptions, transforming a problem statement into a functioning algorithm. This is especially useful in low-code or no-code environments, where users with limited programming expertise can describe a task, and the model generates the corresponding code.

Challenges in this domain include ensuring that the generated code is not only syntactically correct but also logically sound and efficient. Since many code generation models rely heavily on pattern recognition, they may generate correct code in terms of structure but fail to capture the underlying logic or efficiency of the algorithm. Researchers are exploring hybrid models that combine pre-trained Transformers with symbolic reasoning systems to improve the logical consistency and efficiency of generated code.

Transformers and Ethical AI: Reducing Harm and Increasing Transparency

The development of large-scale Transformer models has brought about unprecedented advancements in AI, but it has also raised significant ethical concerns. One of the most pressing issues is the potential for these models to perpetuate harmful biases, spread misinformation, and be misused in malicious ways. As AI systems become more powerful and widely used, it is crucial that ethical considerations are integrated into every stage of model development, from data collection and model training to deployment and monitoring.

The ethical challenges associated with Transformers can be broadly categorized into issues of bias, transparency, and accountability. Bias in AI systems, particularly in large language models, can arise from skewed training data that reflects societal prejudices. These biases are often inadvertently learned by models during training and can manifest in harmful ways, such as reinforcing stereotypes or making discriminatory predictions.

To address these concerns, researchers have been developing methods to **de-bias** large models through techniques like adversarial training, where the model is penalized for generating biased outputs. Additionally, **fairness constraints** can be incorporated into the training process to ensure that models perform equally well across different demographic groups. Another promising approach is **counterfactual reasoning**, which involves asking the model how its predictions would change if certain input variables were different, helping to identify and mitigate biased decision-making.

Transparency is another crucial ethical consideration. Transformers, by their very nature, are complex and opaque, making it difficult for users to understand how a particular output was generated. This lack of interpretability is especially concerning in high-stakes domains like healthcare, law, and finance, where users may rely on AI systems to make critical decisions.

To improve transparency, researchers are working on **explainable AI** (XAI) techniques that can provide insights into the reasoning behind a model's predictions. These techniques aim to make the inner workings of Transformer models more understandable to humans without sacrificing performance.

Moreover, the growing capability of Transformers to generate realistic, convincing content has raised concerns about **misinformation** and **deepfakes**. With the ability to generate text, images, and even videos that mimic real-world data, these models can be exploited to create misleading or harmful content. In response, researchers are exploring methods to detect and mitigate the misuse of AI-generated content, such as **content moderation systems** that can automatically flag harmful outputs and prevent their dissemination.

As AI continues to evolve, ethical considerations will play an increasingly important role in shaping the future of Transformers and other advanced models. By addressing issues of bias, transparency, and accountability, it will be possible to ensure that these powerful tools are used responsibly and for the benefit of society.

Part 4: Building and Training LLMs with Transformers

Part 3 unveiled the magic behind transformers, the engine powering Large Language Models (LLMs). Now, we shift gears and explore the practical aspects of building and training these powerful AI models.

Chapter 7: The Data Behind the Power: Preparing Text Data for LLM Training

Imagine building a house – you need solid materials before construction begins. Similarly, training LLMs requires high-quality data. This chapter dives into the world of data preparation for LLMs.

- **7.1 Data Collection and Preprocessing for Large Language Models:** Just like you wouldn't build a house with random scraps, LLMs need well-structured data. We'll explore how text data is collected from various sources like books, articles, and even the internet. We'll also delve into preprocessing techniques to clean the data, remove irrelevant information, and ensure its quality for optimal LLM training.

- **7.2 Techniques for Handling Large Datasets for Efficient Training:** LLMs thrive on massive amounts of text data. But handling such large datasets can be challenging. This chapter explores techniques for efficiently managing and processing these datasets to ensure smooth and efficient LLM training.

Chapter 8: Training LLMs: Challenges and

Optimization Techniques

Training LLMs is no walk in the park. This chapter dives into the challenges associated with training these complex models.

- **8.1 Challenges of Training Large Language Models:** Computational cost, data bias, and ensuring the model generalizes well to unseen data are some of the hurdles we'll explore. We'll discuss how these challenges can impact the effectiveness and accuracy of LLMs.

- **8.2 Optimization Techniques for Efficient LLM Learning (e.g., Gradient Descent):** Just like training a muscle requires specific techniques, training LLMs relies on optimization algorithms. We'll explore concepts like gradient descent, a technique that helps LLMs learn and improve their performance iteratively.

- **8.3 Fine-Tuning Pre-trained LLMs for Specific Applications:** Imagine having a master chef who can adapt their skills to different cuisines. Similarly, pre-trained LLMs can be fine-tuned for specific tasks. This chapter explores how these pre-trained models can be adapted and customized to excel in various NLP applications.

By understanding data preparation, training challenges, and optimization techniques, you'll gain valuable insights into the real-world process of building and training LLMs. The final part of the book will showcase the exciting possibilities that LLMs unlock and the potential impact they have on our

world.

Part 5: Applications and Future Directions

Get ready to explore the thrilling world of possibilities that Large Language Models (LLMs) unlock! This part showcases the vast applications of LLMs and delves into the exciting future that awaits this technology.

Chapter 9: Unleashing the Power of LLMs: A Range of Applications

LLMs are not just cool research projects; they have the potential to revolutionize various fields. This chapter dives into the diverse applications of LLMs that are shaping our world.

- **9.1 Text Generation and Creative Content Creation:** Imagine a world where AI can write compelling marketing copy, generate realistic dialogue for chatbots, or even create poems or scripts. LLMs are making this a reality! We'll explore how they are being used for creative text generation and content creation across various industries.

- **9.2 Machine Translation: Breaking Down Language Barriers:** Language barriers can be a hindrance to communication and understanding. LLMs are breaking these barriers down! We'll explore how machine translation powered by LLMs is becoming more accurate and nuanced, facilitating communication across languages.

- **9.3 Text Summarization: Extracting Key Information Efficiently:** In today's information overload, efficiently summarizing large amounts of text is crucial. LLMs can be your secret weapon! This chapter explores how they can provide concise and informative summaries of complex documents, articles, or research papers.

- **9.4 Question Answering and Information Retrieval:** Have a burning question? LLMs can be your intelligent assistants! We'll delve into how LLMs are being used to develop powerful question-answering systems, allowing you to retrieve information quickly and accurately.

- **9.5 Additional Applications of LLMs (e.g., Chatbots, Code Generation):** The potential applications of LLMs extend far beyond the examples listed above. We'll explore how LLMs are being used to develop more advanced chatbots that can hold natural conversations, or even generate basic computer code, assisting programmers in their work.

Chapter 10: The Future of LLMs and Transformer Architectures

The world of LLMs and transformer architectures is constantly evolving. This chapter explores the exciting possibilities that lie ahead.

- **10.1 Addressing Biases and Ethical Considerations in LLMs:** As with any powerful technology, ethical considerations are paramount. We'll discuss the potential biases that LLMs might inherit from the data they're trained on and explore how to develop these models responsibly and ethically.

- **10.2 The Future of NLP: Advancements in Transformer Architectures:** Transformer architectures are a work in progress, with researchers constantly pushing the boundaries. We'll explore potential advancements in transformer architectures that could lead to even more powerful and versatile LLMs.

- **10.3 Potential Societal Impacts of Powerful LLMs:** The widespread adoption of LLMs has the potential to significantly impact society. We'll discuss the positive possibilities, such as improved communication and access to information, alongside potential challenges that need to be addressed.

By understanding the applications and future directions of LLMs, you'll gain a well-rounded perspective on this transformative technology. This book has equipped you with the knowledge to navigate the exciting world of LLMs and transformers, opening doors to a future where language processing holds immense potential for progress and innovation.

Sure! Here are 10 case studies of 750 words each that demonstrate the applications, challenges, and solutions involving Large Language Models (LLMs) and

Transformer architectures in real-world scenarios.

---

1. Case Study: Large Language Models in Legal Document Review

Background: The legal industry faces the challenge of reviewing vast amounts of legal documents, which can be time-consuming and resource-intensive. For tasks such as contract review, litigation support, and compliance checks, lawyers and paralegals often need to go through thousands of documents manually. This process is not only slow but also prone to human error. To solve this, a prominent law firm decided to integrate a large language model (LLM) to automate and enhance the review of legal documents.

Problem: The law firm was grappling with a backlog of contracts and litigation documents, some of which spanned hundreds of pages. Reviewing these documents for specific clauses, terms, and legal language required significant manual effort. The task was not only laborious but also required specialized knowledge to ensure compliance with evolving regulations. They needed a tool that could automate the identification of key information, such as clauses, dates, or obligations, and flag potential risks, all while maintaining high accuracy.

Solution: The firm decided to implement a pre-trained transformer model, fine-tuned for the legal domain. They started by using a transformer-based model like BERT (Bidirectional Encoder Representations from Transformers), which had already shown proficiency in understanding complex language structures. To tailor it for legal use, the model was further trained on a corpus of legal documents, including contracts, regulations, and case law.

Fine-tuning was performed on specific legal tasks such as clause extraction, sentiment analysis, and legal obligation identification. By using a supervised learning approach, the model learned to recognize legal jargon, identify specific legal terms, and classify sections based on their relevance to particular legal issues.

Results: After implementing the LLM, the law firm achieved a significant reduction in manual review time. The model was able to extract key clauses, identify conflicting terms, and flag potential legal risks with a high degree of accuracy. This allowed legal professionals to focus on higher-level tasks, such as strategic decision-making, instead of sifting through documents. The model also improved the consistency and accuracy of the review process, ensuring that important information was not overlooked.

Challenges: The biggest challenge was the quality and size of the legal dataset for fine-tuning. Legal documents can be highly specialized and diverse, requiring careful attention to the vocabulary, terminology, and context. Additionally, the model was sometimes prone to misinterpretations of ambiguous legal language, which required human oversight to ensure accuracy. Despite this, the firm saw overall improvements in efficiency and quality.

Conclusion: The integration of LLMs into legal document review processes has transformed the way law firms approach large-scale legal work. The case demonstrates how transformers, when fine-tuned for specialized domains, can offer significant time and cost savings while improving accuracy. As the model continues to learn from more documents, its accuracy and capabilities will further enhance the firm's productivity.

---

2. Case Study: Transformers for Automated Customer Support in E-commerce

Background: An e-commerce giant was facing a significant challenge in handling a growing volume of customer support inquiries. The company's customer support team was overwhelmed with questions related to product inquiries, order tracking, returns, and refunds. Given the scale of the business, managing these inquiries manually was not feasible, leading to long wait times and unsatisfied customers.

Problem: The company needed to scale its customer support operations while ensuring a consistent and timely response. Manually answering queries was inefficient, and existing chatbots had limited success due to their inability to understand complex questions or provide detailed responses.

Solution: The company decided to implement a large language model, specifically GPT-3, for its customer support system. GPT-3, a transformer-based model, was chosen for its ability to generate human-like text and understand a wide range of customer queries.

The first step in the solution was to integrate GPT-3 into a chatbot interface that would handle initial customer queries. The chatbot was trained on previous customer support interactions, FAQs, and product information to give it the necessary context. Fine-tuning was performed to improve the chatbot's performance in handling specific queries related to the company's products, services, and policies.

Results: After implementing GPT-3, the company saw a significant reduction in the number of queries that required human intervention. The chatbot successfully handled a wide range of questions, from order tracking to product details, freeing up customer support agents to focus on more complex issues. The customer satisfaction score improved as response times were drastically reduced, and the chatbot could provide 24/7 support.

The chatbot was also able to escalate complex issues to human agents more efficiently, ensuring that no query was left unresolved. Over time, the model learned to handle an increasing variety of inquiries, improving its performance as it was exposed to more data.

Challenges: Despite the success, there were challenges in the initial deployment. Some customer queries involved complex or specific scenarios that the model struggled to interpret correctly. Additionally, GPT-3 sometimes generated responses that sounded plausible but were factually incorrect, requiring careful monitoring and updates to the training dataset.

Conclusion: By incorporating GPT-3 into its customer support system, the e-commerce company was able to significantly enhance operational efficiency and improve customer satisfaction. This case highlights the potential of transformer-based models in customer service, where their ability to generate contextually relevant and human-like responses is a game-changer.

3. Case Study: Applying Transformers in Healthcare for Patient Data Analysis

Background: A healthcare provider was seeking ways to improve its ability to analyze patient data efficiently. The organization had accumulated a vast amount of unstructured patient records, including medical notes, test results, and radiology reports. These records contained valuable information for diagnosing conditions, recommending treatments, and improving patient outcomes, but they were often buried within large volumes of data.

Problem: Extracting meaningful insights from these unstructured texts manually was not only time-consuming but also inefficient. Traditional data analysis methods were not suitable for handling the scale and complexity of the data. The organization needed an automated solution to sift through the records and extract useful information, such as identifying trends in symptoms, detecting early signs of diseases, and matching patients with appropriate treatments.

Solution: The healthcare provider chose to implement a transformer-based model, specifically BERT, to handle the extraction and analysis of medical data. BERT's bidirectional attention mechanism made it well-suited for understanding context within medical records, where the meaning of certain terms could depend heavily on their surrounding text.

The model was fine-tuned on a dataset of anonymized medical records, including clinical notes and medical literature. Tasks like named entity recognition (NER), symptom identification, and relationship extraction were targeted for fine-tuning. The fine-tuned BERT model was then used to analyze incoming patient data in real time, flagging potential issues and providing recommendations for further examination.

Results: The implementation of the transformer model enabled the healthcare provider to analyze vast amounts of patient data quickly and accurately. BERT was able to identify key medical terms, diagnose potential conditions, and provide recommendations for follow-up care, all while ensuring patient privacy and compliance with healthcare regulations like HIPAA.

Physicians found that the model was an invaluable tool for streamlining their workflow, enabling them to focus on critical decision-making rather than spending hours reviewing data. Early signs of diseases, such as cancer or diabetes, were detected more quickly, leading to faster interventions.

Challenges: One of the challenges faced by the healthcare provider was the domain-specific nature of the medical terminology. The model needed to be finely tuned to the nuances of medical language, which often involved technical terms and abbreviations that were difficult for general-purpose

LLMs to understand. The model also required continuous updates to stay current with the latest medical research and guidelines.

Conclusion: By using transformers to analyze patient data, the healthcare provider significantly improved its ability to extract valuable insights from medical records. The case illustrates the power of LLMs in the healthcare domain, where they can support faster, more accurate diagnoses and improve patient care.

4. Case Study: Financial Market Prediction Using Transformers

Background: A financial services firm wanted to improve its ability to predict stock market trends and financial events using unstructured data sources like news articles, social media posts, and financial reports. The firm faced a challenge in processing the enormous volume of data in real-time and deriving actionable insights to guide investment decisions.

Problem: Traditional quantitative models, which relied solely on numerical data (e.g., historical prices), were insufficient for capturing the sentiment and context that could influence market movements. The company needed a more advanced solution capable of analyzing unstructured textual data to predict stock movements and market trends more effectively.

Solution: The firm chose to integrate a transformer-based model, particularly a fine-tuned version of GPT-3, for natural language processing (NLP) tasks such as sentiment analysis, news summarization, and event extraction. The model was trained to recognize market-related events and financial terms in news articles and social media content, which were then used as features to predict stock price movements.

To improve predictions, the transformer model was trained using a large dataset of historical financial data and associated news stories. The model's attention mechanism allowed it to understand the relationships between market events and price fluctuations, capturing patterns that traditional models could not.

Results: After deploying the transformer model, the company saw a marked improvement in its predictive accuracy. The model was able to predict market movements with greater precision by incorporating both numerical and textual data, which traditional models had previously neglected. Investors were able to make more informed decisions based on real-time analysis of market sentiment, news, and financial reports.

Challenges: Despite the success, the model faced challenges in dealing with noisy or contradictory data, such as conflicting news reports or social media trends that were not always reliable. Moreover, market events are influenced by complex, global factors, which made predictions difficult at times.

Conclusion: By combining the power of transformer models with traditional financial analysis, the firm was able to enhance its market prediction capabilities. This case demonstrates the potential for transformers to improve decision-making in the financial sector by processing and analyzing both structured and unstructured data.

---

5. Case Study: Using Transformers for Content Generation in Marketing

Background: A marketing agency was tasked with creating high volumes of engaging content for a variety of clients in different industries. Producing this content manually was slow, and the agency needed a way to automate the process without sacrificing quality. The agency faced challenges in maintaining creativity while ensuring that the generated content was aligned with brand guidelines and resonated with target audiences.

Problem: The agency was producing content like blog posts, social media updates, and email campaigns for clients across several sectors, but the process was time-consuming. Moreover, keeping up with evolving trends and ensuring consistency in tone and style for each client was difficult.

Solution: The marketing agency implemented GPT-3, a transformer-based model, to generate content automatically. By fine-tuning GPT-3 on a corpus of industry-specific content, the agency was able to teach the model how to produce relevant and high-quality material for each client. The model was set up to write in different tones and styles based on client preferences.

The agency also integrated the model with a content management system (CMS), allowing clients to provide brief prompts that would guide the model's content creation. This streamlined the process, enabling the agency to produce articles and posts more efficiently.

Results: GPT-3 was able to generate high-quality content that aligned with each client's brand voice and tone. The agency saw a 40% reduction in time spent creating content, which allowed them to take on more clients. The content generated by GPT-3 also led to higher engagement on social media and increased traffic to clients' websites.

Challenges: Despite the success, the model sometimes produced content that lacked deep insights or creativity, which required human editing. The team also needed to ensure that the content was free from plagiarism and aligned with SEO best practices.

Conclusion: The implementation of GPT-3 in content generation helped the agency save time and improve the scale of its operations. The case demonstrates how transformers can be leveraged in the marketing industry to automate creative processes while maintaining quality and brand consistency.

6. Case Study: Personalizing E-Commerce Recommendations with Transformers

Background: An e-commerce platform was facing challenges in offering personalized recommendations to its users. While basic recommendation systems based on user behavior and product categorization were in place, they struggled to deliver highly personalized, context-aware suggestions that could lead to higher conversion rates. The platform needed a more sophisticated solution to enhance its product recommendation engine.

Problem: Despite having a large user base, the platform's recommendation system failed to capture the nuance of individual customer preferences.

Recommendations were based mostly on simple metrics like browsing history and purchase frequency, which often led to irrelevant suggestions that did not increase user engagement or sales. The platform wanted to incorporate a more dynamic, personalized approach to recommendations, considering user-specific preferences, seasonal trends, and contextual factors.

Solution: The platform integrated a transformer-based model (BERT) to power its recommendation system. The model was fine-tuned on historical user data, including previous purchases, browsing history, product interactions, and even product descriptions. The key was to leverage the power of BERT's attention mechanism, allowing the system to consider the entire context of user behavior to predict what a customer might be interested in next. Additionally, the model was trained to understand text-based attributes of the products, such as features, category, and brand names, making the recommendation more context-aware.

Results: The implementation of the transformer-based recommendation system led to significant improvements in engagement and conversion rates. Users started receiving more relevant and personalized product suggestions, with an increase in average order value and purchase frequency. The system also became better at predicting seasonal trends, providing users with timely recommendations based on their preferences and historical patterns.

Challenges: One of the challenges the platform faced was ensuring that the model was capable of handling the dynamic nature of e-commerce, where trends can change rapidly. To address this, the team continuously retrained the model with updated user data and new product features to maintain its relevance. Additionally, the model's computational cost posed challenges, as the attention mechanism required substantial resources to process large volumes of user interactions in real-time.

Conclusion: The case study illustrates how transformers, such as BERT, can dramatically improve personalized recommendations in e-commerce. By understanding complex user behavior and contextual product data, the platform was able to deliver more relevant and timely suggestions, which led to higher user engagement and improved sales performance.

7. Case Study: Enhancing Healthcare Diagnostics with Transformer Models

Background: A healthcare startup specializing in radiology was developing an AI-powered tool to assist doctors in diagnosing medical conditions from X-rays, MRIs, and CT scans. Although existing AI tools had made strides in image recognition, the startup wanted to improve the model's diagnostic accuracy by incorporating radiology reports and patient histories—unstructured textual data that could provide important context for the images.

Problem: The radiology tool struggled with integrating the textual data from medical records with the images. While the image recognition component was fairly accurate, it was not able to fully comprehend the clinical history, symptoms, and context provided in the radiology reports. The company wanted to create a solution that could analyze both the visual and textual data to provide a more comprehensive diagnosis.

Solution: The startup turned to transformer models like BERT to combine the textual information from patient records with the visual data from scans. The team fine-tuned the model on a dataset containing clinical reports, X-ray images, and diagnostic labels. The transformer model was used to analyze and extract key medical terms from the reports and match them with the visual features of the images. This allowed the model to offer a more holistic diagnosis, taking into account both textual and visual inputs.

Results: The integration of the transformer-based model significantly improved the diagnostic tool's accuracy. By considering both textual and image data, the model was able to detect diseases and conditions that had been overlooked by traditional models. It also enabled the system to suggest possible next steps for further testing or treatment, improving the overall efficiency of the healthcare process. Doctors found the tool invaluable for providing second opinions and confirming diagnoses.

Challenges: The primary challenge was the complexity of training the model to understand the nuanced medical language and integrate it effectively with visual features. The dataset had to be carefully curated to ensure that the text and image data were correctly aligned. Additionally, ensuring that the model adhered to strict privacy and regulatory standards (e.g., HIPAA) was a significant concern.

Conclusion: This case study demonstrates how combining textual and visual data using transformer models can revolutionize healthcare diagnostics. By incorporating both structured and unstructured data, the AI tool was able to offer a more accurate and comprehensive diagnosis, which can improve patient care and reduce diagnostic errors.

8. Case Study: Automating Code Review with Transformers

Background: A software development company faced challenges in maintaining the quality of its codebase due to the rapid pace of development and frequent code updates. The manual code review process was time-consuming and error-prone, leading to issues with inconsistent coding standards and missed bugs. The company wanted to automate the code review process while ensuring that the code met quality standards.

Problem: With a growing team of developers, it became increasingly difficult to manually review each line of code for compliance with best practices, security vulnerabilities, and potential bugs. Traditional linting tools were not sufficient because they only focused on syntax and did not account for the more complex logic and potential bugs in the code. The company needed a solution that could automatically review code for both quality and functionality.

Solution: The company implemented a transformer-based model, such as GPT-3, for automated code review. The model was fine-tuned on a large dataset of code from open-source projects and internal repositories. It was trained to identify issues like coding style violations, logical errors, security vulnerabilities, and even suggest improvements. The model also incorporated contextual understanding, enabling it to provide feedback on the overall design and structure of the code.

Results: The transformer-based code review system dramatically reduced the time spent on manual reviews. Developers were able to receive instant feedback on their code, which improved the speed of development and reduced the number of bugs and vulnerabilities in production code. The system also helped maintain consistency in coding standards across the entire development team.

Challenges: While the model performed well in most cases, it struggled with highly specialized codebases or complex algorithms that required deep domain knowledge. Additionally, the model's feedback was sometimes overly generic or inaccurate, requiring human oversight to refine suggestions.

Conclusion: This case study highlights the potential of using transformer models to automate the code review process, significantly improving development speed and code quality. Although there are challenges in specialized contexts, the automation of code reviews with LLMs can be a valuable tool for modern software development teams.

9. Case Study: Legal Document Summarization and Analysis

Background: A law firm was handling a large number of legal contracts, case law documents, and regulatory filings. These documents were often lengthy and complex, requiring hours of manual review to extract key details and identify relevant sections. The firm sought an AI solution that could automate the summarization and analysis of these documents, improving efficiency and ensuring accuracy.

Problem: Manual review of legal documents was not only time-consuming but also error-prone, especially given the legal jargon and the length of some contracts. The firm's attorneys needed a way to quickly extract important clauses, terms, and conditions from lengthy documents, reducing the time spent on document analysis and allowing them to focus on higher-value tasks.

Solution: The law firm implemented a transformer-based model like BERT, fine-tuned for legal text analysis and summarization. The model was trained on a large dataset of legal documents, including contracts, case laws, and legal memos. It was designed to identify key clauses, summarize legal arguments, and even extract relevant precedents from case law. This helped the attorneys focus on critical sections of documents without having to read everything in detail.

Results: The transformer model significantly reduced the time spent on document analysis. Attorneys could quickly generate summaries of long legal documents and identify relevant clauses in a fraction of the time it would take to do manually. The model was able to identify and flag potential risks and inconsistencies in contracts, ensuring higher accuracy and reducing human error.

Challenges: The main challenge was the complexity of the legal language. The model had to be specifically trained to understand the intricacies of legal terminology, which is often different from everyday language. Additionally, there was a need to constantly update the model to reflect new legal precedents and changes in regulations.

Conclusion: This case study shows how transformer-based models can be applied to legal text analysis and summarization, reducing the time spent on document review while improving accuracy and efficiency. Fine-tuning models for domain-specific languages, like legal jargon, is critical to achieving optimal results in specialized industries.

10. Case Study: AI-Powered Fraud Detection in Financial Transactions

Background: A global bank was seeking to improve its fraud detection system to identify suspicious transactions in real-time. The bank's existing rule-based system was reactive, catching only a small percentage of fraudulent activities. They wanted to implement a proactive AI-based system capable of analyzing transaction data and identifying anomalies that could indicate fraud.

Problem: Traditional fraud detection systems relied on predefined rules and thresholds, which were insufficient for identifying new, evolving fraudulent activities. The bank faced the challenge of detecting emerging patterns of fraud that did not fit existing rules or trends. The system needed to be capable of identifying subtle, complex patterns and flagging potential fraud in real-time.

Solution: The bank turned to transformer-based models, such as GPT-3, to analyze large volumes of transaction data. The model was trained on historical transaction records, including both legitimate and fraudulent transactions. The transformer architecture allowed the model to detect complex patterns of fraud that might not have been captured by traditional methods. The model was integrated into the bank's real-time transaction monitoring system, providing instant alerts for suspicious activities.

Results: The new AI-powered fraud detection system significantly improved the bank's ability to identify fraudulent transactions. By leveraging the transformer model's contextual analysis and attention mechanism, the system was able to detect even subtle fraud patterns that had previously gone unnoticed. The bank saw a reduction in false positives, and the rate of successfully intercepted fraud increased by 35%.

Challenges: One challenge was ensuring that the model could operate in real-time without compromising speed or accuracy. Additionally, the model required continuous retraining to adapt to new methods of fraud as they emerged.

Conclusion: This case study illustrates how transformer models can be effectively applied in fraud detection by identifying complex, evolving patterns in financial data. By leveraging deep learning techniques, the bank was able to significantly improve its fraud detection capabilities, offering a more secure experience for customers and reducing financial losses.